EASY SMOKER COOKBOOK

THE EFFORTLESS CHEF SERIES

VOL. IV

By
Chef Maggie Chow
Copyright © 2015 by Saxonberg Associates
All rights reserved

Published by
BookSumo, a division of Saxonberg Associates
http://www.booksumo.com/

A Gift From Me To You...

I know you like cultural food. But what about Japanese Sushi?

Join my private mailing list of readers and get a copy of *Infinite Sushi: A Complete Set of Sushi and Japanese Recipes* by fellow BookSumo author Hashimoto Kazuma for FREE!

http://booksumo.com/easy-smoothie-cookbook/

Enjoy some of the best sushi available!

You will also receive updates about all my new books when they are free. So please show your support.

Also don't forget to like and subscribe on the social networks. I love meeting my readers. Links to all my profiles are below so please click and connect :)

Facebook

Twitter

INTRODUCTION

Welcome to *The Effortless Chef Series*! Thank you for taking the time to download the *Easy Smoothie Cookbook*.

Come take a journey with me into the delights of easy cooking. The point of this cookbook and all my cookbooks is to exemplify the effortless nature of cooking simply.

The *Easy Smoothie Cookbook* is about smoothies.

Smoothies are great as desserts and even as full course meals. In this book we focus on smoothies as desserts. You will find that even though the recipes are simple, the taste of the drinks are quite amazing.

So will you join me in an adventure of simple cooking? If the answer is yes (and I hope it is) please consult the table of contents to find the drinks you are most interested in. Once you are ready jump right in and start cooking.

— Chef Maggie Chow

TABLE OF CONTENTS

Introduction 4
Table of Contents..5
Contact Me 7
NOTICE TO PRINT READERS: 8
Legal Notes 9
A Smoothie for The Groovies 10
Peanut Chocolate Banana Smoothie 11
West Coast Smoothie 12
Eastern European Smoothie 13
Easy Blueberry Smoothie...14
Melon Madness Smoothie 15
Cinnamon & Pear Smoothie 16
Peanut Chocolate Banana Smoothie II 17
Grapefruit Smoothie 18
Best Friends Smoothie...19
Amaretto Smoothie..20
Ethiopian Inspired Smoothie.....................................21
American Muscle Smoothie 22
Smoothie Pops..23

Tofuberry Smoothie 24
Floridian Smoothie 25
Gator Smoothies 26
Sour Smoothie 27
Orange & Ginger Smoothie 28
Polynesian Smoothie 29
Eggnog Smoothie 30
Veggie Smoothie 31
Pacific Smoothie 33
Maggie's Favorite Smoothie 34
Cranberry Smoothie 35
A GIFT FROM ME TO YOU... 36
Come On... 38
Let's Be Friends :) 38
About The Publisher. 39
Can I Ask A Favour? 40
INTERESTED IN OTHER EASY COOKBOOKS? 41

CONTACT ME

If you find that something important to you is missing from this book please contact me at maggie@booksumo.com.

I will try my best to re-publish a revised copy taking your feedback into consideration and let you know when the book has been revised with you in mind.

:)

— Chef Maggie Chow

NOTICE TO PRINT READERS:

Hey, because you purchased the print version of this book you are entitled to its original digital version for free by Amazon.

So when you have the time, please review your purchases, and download the Kindle version of this book.

You might enjoy consuming this book more in its original digital format.

;)

But, in any case, take care and enjoy reading in whatever format you choose!

LEGAL NOTES

ALL RIGHTS RESERVED. NO PART OF THIS BOOK MAY BE REPRODUCED OR TRANSMITTED IN ANY FORM OR BY ANY MEANS. PHOTOCOPYING, POSTING ONLINE, AND / OR DIGITAL COPYING IS STRICTLY PROHIBITED UNLESS WRITTEN PERMISSION IS GRANTED BY THE BOOK'S PUBLISHING COMPANY. LIMITED USE OF THE BOOK'S TEXT IS PERMITTED FOR USE IN REVIEWS WRITTEN FOR THE PUBLIC AND/OR PUBLIC DOMAIN.

A Smoothie for The Groovies

Ingredients

1. 2 small bananas, broken into chunks
2. 1 cup frozen unsweetened strawberries
3. 1 (8 oz) container vanilla low-fat yogurt
4. 3/4 cup milk

Directions

1. Take out the ingredients mentioned above and put them in a blender
2. Blend these ingredients until you find them smooth
3. Serve by pouring this smoothie into a glass.

Serving: 2

Timing Information:

Preparation	Cooking	Total Time
5 mins		5 mins

Peanut Chocolate Banana Smoothie

Ingredients

1. Banana, sliced
2. half cup skim milk
3. 2 tbsps peanut butter
4. 2 tbsps chocolate syrup

Directions

1. Place all the ingredients mentioned above in a blender and blend it until the mixture is smooth.
2. Serve by pouring this smoothie into a glass.

Serving: 1

Timing Information:

Preparation	Cooking	Total Time
5 mins		5 mins

WEST COAST SMOOTHIE

Ingredients

1. 7 large strawberries
2. 1 (8 oz) container lemon yogurt
3. 1/3 cup orange juice

Directions

1. Take out the strawberries and place them in a plastic container
2. Put this container in the freezer for an hour
3. Now take the strawberries and other ingredients, and put them in a blender
4. Blend ingredients together until smooth
5. Pour smoothie into a tall glass and serve.

Serving: 1

Timing Information:

Preparation	Cooking	Total Time
10 mins		1 hr 10 mins

Eastern European Smoothie

Ingredients

1. 6 fluid oz vodka
2. 18 fluid oz
3. orange juice 1 cup
4. frozen strawberries
5. 4 scoops orange sherbet
6. 1 cup crushed ice

Directions

1. Take out the ingredients and put them in a blender
2. Blend all ingredients until smooth
3. Pour smoothie in an appropriate glass of your choice and serve

Serving: 4

Timing Information:

Preparation	Cooking	Total Time
10 mins		10 mins

Easy Blueberry Smoothie

Ingredients

1. 1 1/4 cup Ocean Spray Blueberry Juice Cocktail, chilled
2. 3/4 cup Ocean Spray Fresh Blueberries, cleaned and rinsed
3. 1 cup vanilla yogurt or vanilla frozen yogurt

Directions

1. Take out blueberry juice cocktail and blueberries initially
2. Blend them together until you see that the mixture is smooth
3. Take one cup of vanilla yoghurt and blend it together with the previous mixture.
4. Now serve by pouring this smoothie into a glass

Serving: 4

Timing Information:

Preparation	Cooking	Total Time
5 mins		5 mins

Melon Madness Smoothie

Ingredients

1. ¼ cantaloupe - peeled, seeded and cubed
2. ¼ honeydew melon - peeled, seeded and cubed
3. 1 lime, juiced
4. 2 tbsps sugar

Directions

1. Take out the ingredients mentioned above and put them in a blender
2. Blend all ingredients until you find them smooth
3. Now serve the smoothie in a glass

Serving: 4

Timing Information:

Preparation	Cooking	Total Time
5 mins		5 mins

Cinnamon & Pear Smoothie

Ingredients

1. 2 pears, quartered and cores removed
2. 1 banana, cut in chunks
3. 1 cup milk
4. half cup vanilla yogurt
5. half tsp ground cinnamon
6. 1 pinch ground nutmeg

Directions

1. Take out the ingredients mentioned above and put them in a blender
2. Blend all the ingredients until you find them smooth
3. Now serve the smoothie in a glass.

Serving: 2

Timing Information:

Preparation	Cooking	Total Time
10 mins		10 mins

Peanut Chocolate Banana Smoothie II

Ingredients

1. 2 cups ice
2. 2 cups chocolate soy milk
3. 1 large banana
4. 2 tbsps creamy peanut butter, or more to taste

Directions

1. Take out the ingredients mentioned above and put them in a blender
2. Blend these ingredients until you find them smooth
3. Serve and enjoy.

Serving size: 2

Timing Information:

Preparation	Cooking	Total Time
10 mins		10 mins

GRAPEFRUIT SMOOTHIE

Ingredients

1. 3 grapefruit, peeled and sectioned
2. 1 cup cold water
3. 3 oz fresh spinach
4. 6 ice cubes
5. 1 (half inch) piece peeled fresh ginger
6. 1 tsp flax seeds

Directions

1. Take out the ingredients mentioned above and put them in a blender
2. Blend these ingredients until you find them smooth
3. Serve and enjoy.

Serving size: 2

Timing Information:

Preparation	Cooking	Total Time
10 mins		10 mins

Best Friends Smoothie

Ingredients

1. 1 cup frozen strawberries
2. 1 cup plain Greek yogurt
3. 1 cup frozen mango chunks
4. half cup 1% milk
5. 1 scoop vanilla whey protein powder
6. 5 fresh mint leaves, or more to taste

Directions

1. At first, blend together strawberries, protein powder, mango, Greek yoghurt and milk until you find that you have reached the required smoothness
2. Now add mint leaves and pulse until the leaves are chopped.
3. Serve in a glass.

Serving size: 2

Timing Information:

Preparation	Cooking	Total Time
10 mins		10 mins

AMARETTO SMOOTHIE

Ingredients

1. 4 (1.5 fluid oz) jiggers amaretto liqueur
2. 4 (1.5 fluid oz) jiggers milk
3. 1 cup vanilla ice cream

Directions

1. Take out the ingredients mentioned above and put them in a blender
2. Blend these ingredients until you find them smooth
3. Serve the smoothie in a glass containing some ice.

Serving size: 4

Timing Information:

Preparation	Cooking	Total Time
10 mins		10 mins

Ethiopian Inspired Smoothie

Ingredients

1. 1 cup crushed ice
2. 3/4 cup coconut milk
3. 1/4 cup brewed coffee
4. 3 tbsps raw sugar (such as Sugar in the Raw)
5. 1 tbsp hot chocolate mix
6. 1 tbsp vanilla extract

Directions

1. Take out the ingredients mentioned above and put them in a blender
2. Blend these ingredients until you find them smooth
3. Serve and enjoy.

Serving size: 3

Timing Information:

Preparation	Cooking	Total Time
10 mins		10 mins

American Muscle Smoothie

Ingredients

1. 1 cup almond milk
2. half cup fresh papaya
3. 1 scoop protein powder
4. 1 (1 inch) piece peeled and chopped fresh turmeric root
5. 1 (half inch) piece fresh ginger root, peeled
6. 3 cubes ice, or as desired

Directions

1. Take out the ingredients except ice cubes that are mentioned above and put them in a blender
2. Blend these ingredients until smooth
3. Now add ice cubes and blend again. Enjoy.

Serving size: 1

Timing Information:

Preparation	Cooking	Total Time
10 mins		10 mins

Smoothie Pops

Ingredients

1. 1 cup hulled strawberries
2. 1 cup fresh blueberries
3. 1 cup fresh raspberries
4. 1 cup Greek yogurt
5. 5 (1 gram) packets stevia powder
6. half tsp vanilla extract

Directions

1. Take out the ingredients mentioned above and put them in a blender
2. Blend these ingredients until you find them smooth
3. Pour the prepared mixture into a 12 ice pop mold and also insert some sticks or handles of some kind.
4. Freeze this mixture for about 4 hours.
5. Serve and Enjoy.

Serving size: 3

Timing Information:

Preparation	Cooking	Total Time
10 mins		10 mins

Tofuberry Smoothie

Ingredients

1. 1/4 cup diced silken tofu
2. 2 tbsps soy milk
3. 1/4 cup fruit yogurt
4. half cup raspberries
5. 1/4 banana
6. 2 cups orange juice

Directions

1. Take out the ingredients mentioned above and put them in a blender
2. Blend these ingredients until you find them smooth
3. Serve the smoothie in a glass having some ice or vanilla ice cream.

Serving size: 3

Timing Information:

Preparation	Cooking	Total Time
7 mins		7 mins

FLORIDIAN SMOOTHIE

Ingredients

1. 1 cup strawberries
2. half cup bananas, sliced
3. half cup fresh raspberries
4. half cup strawberry yogurt
5. 1 tbsp powdered lemonade mix
6. half cup ice cubes
7. 2 fluid oz of each: vodka, rum, whiskey
8. 2 fluid oz cherry vodka (such as UV Red)

Directions

1. Initially place yoghurt, bananas, lemonade mix, raspberries, strawberries and some ice cubes into a blender.
2. Blend until smooth.
3. Combine with mixture vodka, rum, whiskey and cherry vodka, continue blending.
4. Serve this smoothie in two large glasses

Serving size: 2

Timing Information:

Preparation	Cooking	Total Time
10 mins		10 mins

Gator Smoothies

Ingredients

1. 2 cups ice
2. 2 cups grape flavored sports drink
3. 2 scoops vanilla ice cream

Directions

1. Take out the ingredients mentioned above and put them in a blender
2. Blend these ingredients until you find them smooth
3. Serve and enjoy.

Serving size: 2

Timing Information:

Preparation	Cooking	Total Time
5 mins		5 mins

SOUR SMOOTHIE

Ingredients

1. 1 cup ice cubes
2. 1 orange, peeled
3. 2 limes, peeled
4. 1 lemon, peeled
5. 1 kiwi, peeled
6. 1 tsp honey, or more to taste

Directions

1. Take out the ingredients mentioned above and put them in a blender
2. Blend these ingredients until you find them smooth
3. Serve and enjoy.

Serving size: 2

Timing Information:

Preparation	Cooking	Total Time
10 mins		10 mins

Orange & Ginger Smoothie

Ingredients

1. 1 orange, peeled
2. 2 carrots, peeled and cut into chunks
3. half cup red grapes
4. half cup ice cubes
5. 1/4 cup water
6. 1 (1 inch) piece peeled fresh ginger

Directions

1. Take out the ingredients mentioned above and put them in a blender
2. Blend these ingredients until you find them smooth
3. Serve and enjoy.

Serving size: 1

Timing Information:

Preparation	Cooking	Total Time
10 mins		10 mins

POLYNESIAN SMOOTHIE

Ingredients

1. 1 cup ice
2. 2 cups pineapple juice
3. half cup ginger ale
4. 3 tbsps coconut milk
5. 1 tbsp white sugar

Directions

1. Take out the ingredients mentioned above and put them in a blender
2. Blend these ingredients until you find them smooth
3. Serve and enjoy.

Serving size: 3

Timing Information:

Preparation	Cooking	Total Time
5 mins		5 mins

EGGNOG SMOOTHIE

Ingredients

1. 1 quart eggnog
2. 1 (5.1 oz) package instant vanilla pudding mix
3. 1 (12 oz) container frozen whipped topping
4. half cup rum, or amount desired

Directions

1. Take out the eggnog and put it into a mixing bowl
2. Now add pudding mix, rum and whipped topping into this eggnog and blend it together.
3. Now cover this mixture and place it into a refrigerator for about 2 hours
4. Serve it chilled.

Serving size: 8

Timing Information:

Preparation	Cooking	Total Time
10 mins	2 hrs	2 hr 10 mins

Veggie Smoothie

Ingredients

1. 1/3 cup of each: broccoli florets, cauliflower florets, baby carrots, blueberries
2. 1 tbsp chia seeds
3. 1 tbsp honey
4. half lime, peeled
5. 1 stalk celery
6. half raw beet, peeled
7. 1 cup fresh spinach
8. half orange, peeled
9. 1 cup water, or as desired

Directions

1. Take out the ingredients mentioned above and put them in a blender but the water needs to be in the blender first
2. Blend ingredients at high speed until smooth
3. Serve and enjoy.

Serving size: 1

Timing Information:

| Preparation | Cooking | Total Time |

10 mins		10 mins

PACIFIC SMOOTHIE

Ingredients

1. 10 ice cubes
2. 1 banana
3. 4 tsps maple syrup
4. 4 tsps brown sugar
5. 1 cup eggnog
6. 1/4 cup orange juice
7. 1/4 cup vanilla yogurt

Directions

1. Take out the ingredients mentioned above and put them in a blender
2. Blend these ingredients until you find them smooth
3. Serve and enjoy.

Serving size: 1
Timing Information:

Preparation	Cooking	Total Time
5 mins		5 mins

Maggie's Favorite Smoothie

Ingredients

1. 1 banana
2. 1/4 cup frozen blueberries
3. 3/4 cup frozen peach slices
4. 1/4 cup yogurt
5. 2 tbsps all fruit blueberry syrup
6. 1/8 cup rice milk

Directions

1. First, you need to blend all the ingredients except the rice milk until the mixture is smooth
2. Now add rice milk and continue blending.
3. Pour this smoothie in a glass and enjoy.

Serving size: 3
Timing Information:

Preparation	Cooking	Total Time
10 mins		10 mins

Cranberry Smoothie

Ingredients

1. 1 cup almond milk
2. 1 banana
3. half cup frozen mixed berries
4. half cup fresh cranberries

Directions

1. Take out the ingredients mentioned above and put them in a blender
2. Blend the ingredients until you find them smooth
3. Put this mixture in the refrigerator for about 1 hour to get it chilled
4. Now serve the smoothie and enjoy.

Serving size: 2
Timing Information:

Preparation	Cooking	Total Time
10 mins		1 hr 10 mins

A GIFT FROM ME TO YOU...

I know you like cultural food. But what about Japanese Sushi?

Join my private mailing list of readers and get a copy of *Infinite Sushi: A Complete Set of Sushi and Japanese Recipes* by fellow BookSumo author Hashimoto Kazuma for FREE!

http://booksumo.com/easy-smoothie-cookbook/

Enjoy some of the best sushi available!

You will also receive updates about all my new books when they are free. So please show your support.

Also don't forget to like and subscribe on the social networks. I love meeting my readers. Links to all my profiles are below so please click and connect :)

Facebook

Twitter

Come On...
Let's Be Friends :)

I adore my readers and love connecting with them socially. Please follow the links below so we can connect on Facebook, Twitter, and Google+.

[Facebook](#)

[Twitter](#)

I also have a blog that I regularly update for my readers so check it out below.

[My Blog](#)

ABOUT THE PUBLISHER.

BookSumo specializes in providing the best books on special topics that you care about. *The Easy Smoothie Cookbook* is an amazing collection of simple smoothie recipes.

To find out more about BookSumo and find other books we have written go to:

http://booksumo.com/.

Can I Ask A Favour?

If you found this book interesting, or have otherwise found any benefit in it. Then may I ask that you post a review of it on Amazon? Nothing excites me more than new reviews, especially reviews which suggest new topics for writing. I do read all reviews and I always factor feedback into my newer works.

So if you are willing to take ten minutes to write what you sincerely thought about this book then please visit our Amazon page and post your opinions.

Again thank you!

Interested in Other Easy Cookbooks?

Everything is easy check out some of my other cookbooks:

Grilling:

Easy Grilling Cookbook

Nutella

Easy Nutella Cookbook

Filipino Cuisine:

Easy Filipino Cookbook

Quiche:

Easy Quiche Cookbook

Burgers:

Easy Burger Cookbook

Printed in Great Britain
by Amazon